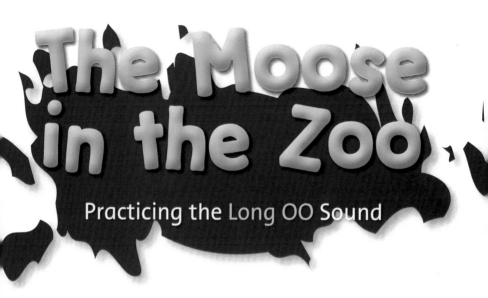

The Moose in the Zoo

Practicing the Long OO Sound

Rafael Moya

Rosen
PHONICS
READERS

Rosen
Classroom™

T0019171

This is Bruno.
Bruno is a moose!

Bruno is the star of the zoo.

Bruno loves June.
June is a zookeeper.

June brings Bruno food.

June takes Bruno to a pool.

June fixes Bruno's roof.
She uses her tools.

June leaves Bruno at noon.
"I'll be back soon!" says June.

Bruno makes a hole in his gate.

A moose is on the loose!

June finds Bruno at the pool.

"You know the rules, Bruno!
Back to the zoo."